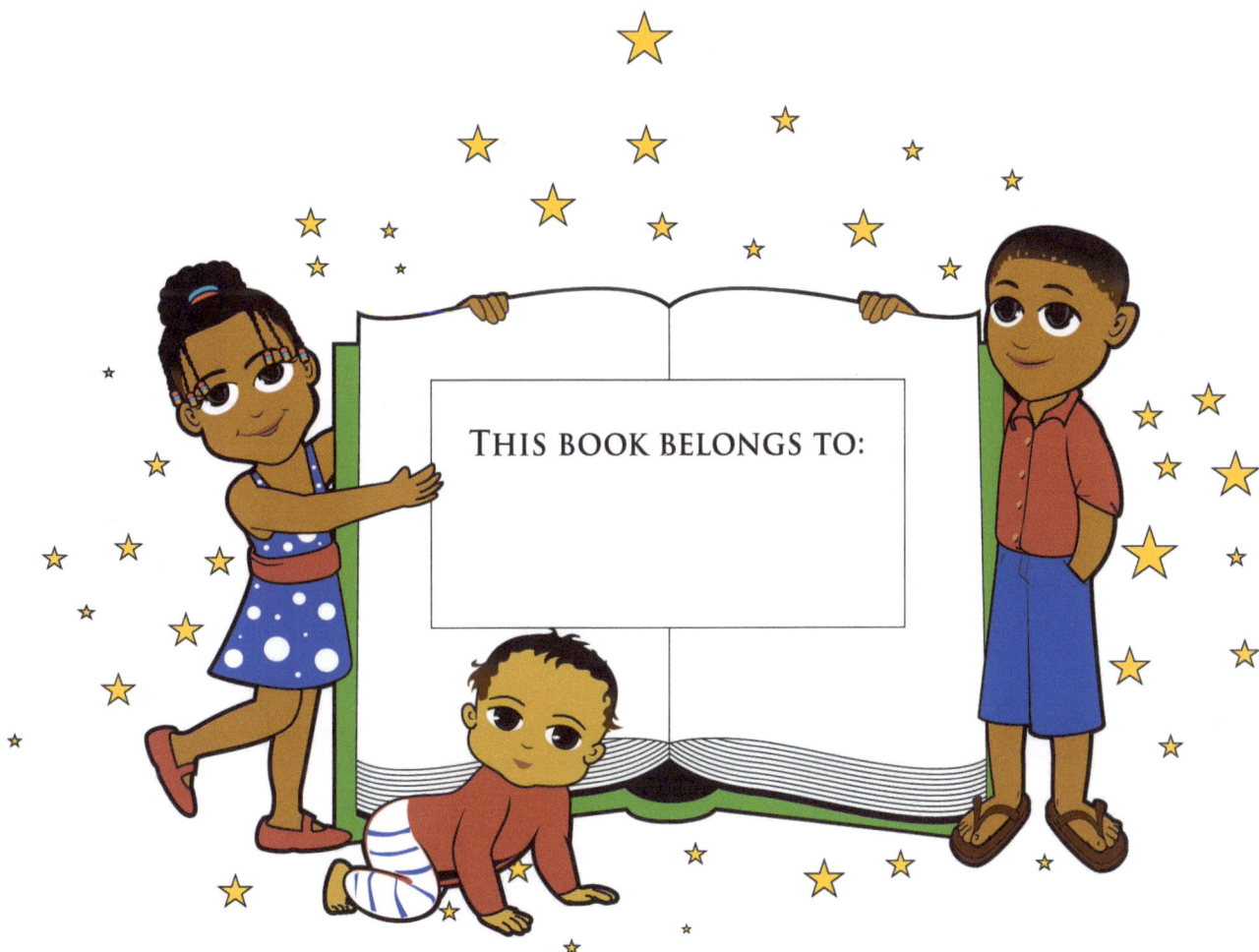

This book belongs to:

To my Super Mom, Ethel Nadiyah.
~Z.C.

**MyLO**
**PUBLISHING**

Library of Congress Control Number: 2016921326
ISBN: 978-0-9910341-2-3

BY Zarinah Curry

# Super Mom®

## Travels To London

Chapter 1

Let's Plan A Team Mission!

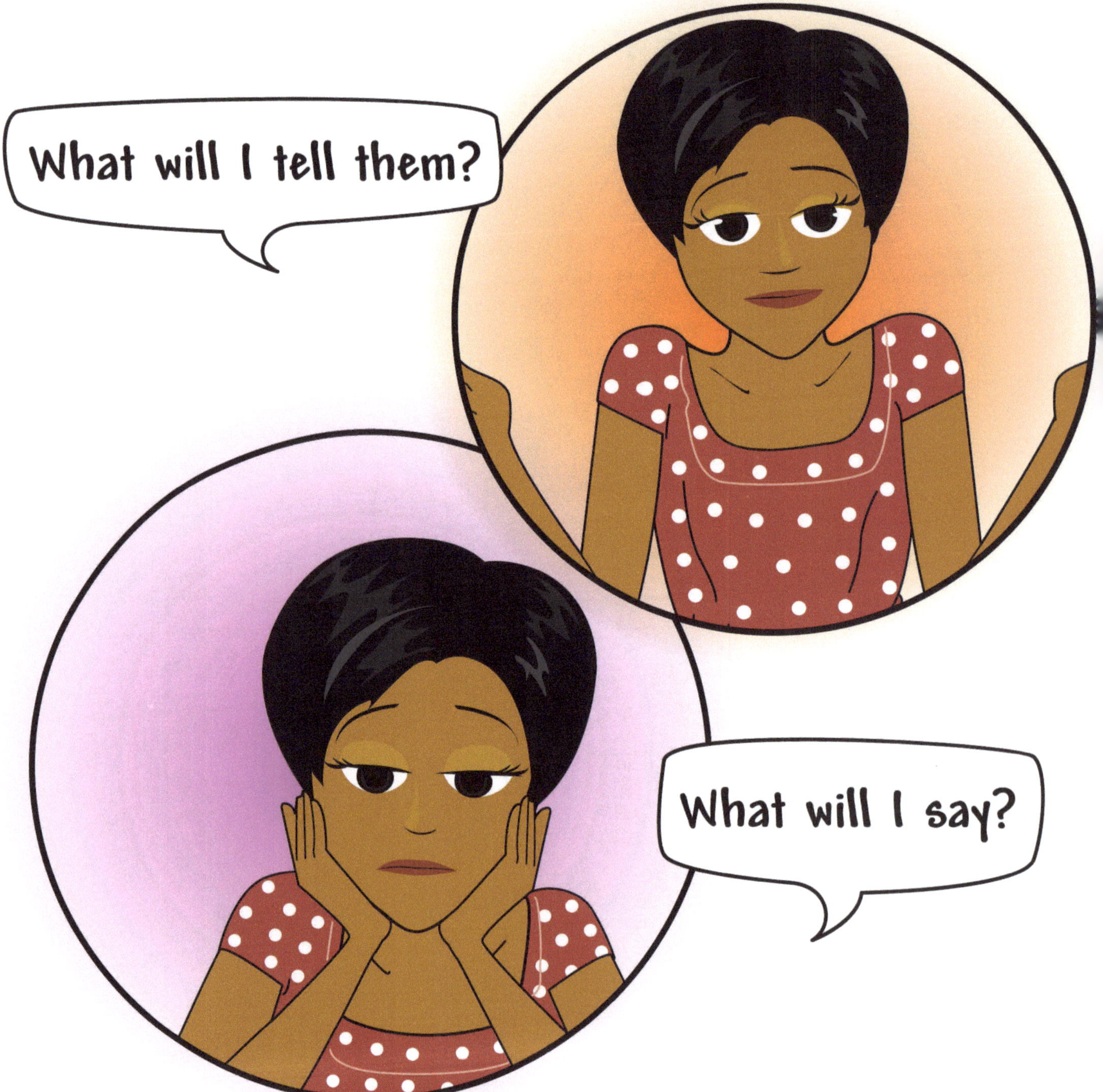
What will I tell them?
What will I say?

Let's plan a team mission to a magical place. We'll create great memories that cannot be replaced.
Super Mom
We will send you as an explorer to this faraway land and tell the kids you will learn as much as you can.

Mom, please don't go.
We want you to stay.
Who will braid my hair
and help choose my
clothes for the next day?

Don't worry Kids.
Do not shed a tear.
I need to go, but
Dad will stay here.

In London, I will meet people from around the globe. When I come home, I'll share stories that you have never been told.

Visit a castle!
See the Queen!

Try fish and chips
when you dine...at nine!

## Team Mission

Explorer: Mom

Destination: London

Transportation: Airplane

Length of Trip: 5 Days

Team Name: _____ ???

What team name would you create for your family?

Hello, London!

Chapter 2

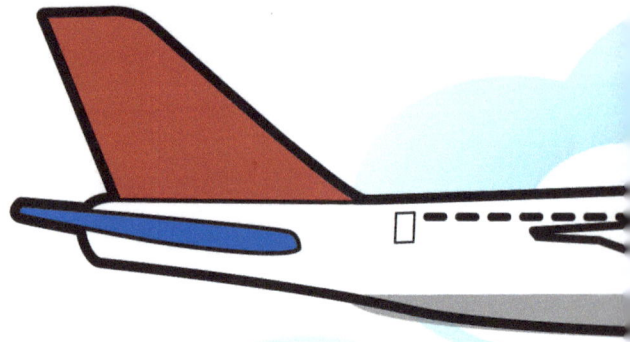

# Day 1

# Day 2

# Day 3

# Day 4

I have one more day to sightsee and explore.

It's been a few days since I've been away. I will see you and the Kids in less than one da

We look forward to seeing you.
Please don't be late.
Call us when you arrive
at the airport gate.

# Home Sweet Home!

Chapter 3

I saw Windsor Castle, Big Ben and Buckingham Palace, too.
I went to the theater and ate fish and chips... not at nine, but at noon.

There are so many landmarks that I did not get to see.
Next time I travel to London, I want you all to come with me.

Tower Bridge
London Eye Abbey Road
British Museum Big Ben
Buckingham Palace Hyde Park
Royal Opera House
London Zoo Kensington Palace
Shakespeare's Globe Theater
Wembley Stadium
Tower of London
The British Library

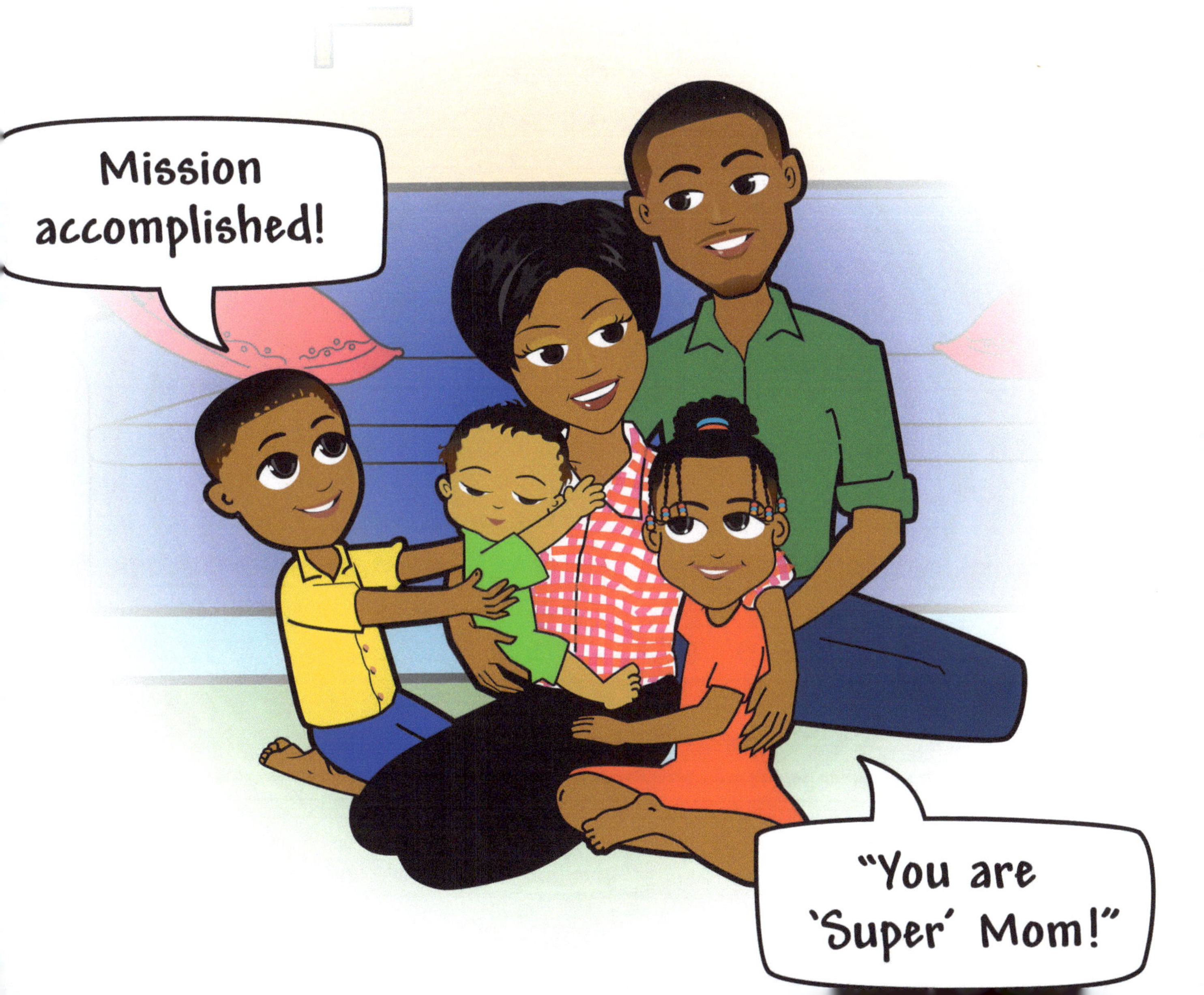
Mission accomplished!
"You are 'Super' Mom!"

The End

#SuperMom

Curry Family, July 2013
Scottsdale, Arizona

Photo by: Moms at Heart Photography

www.ingramcontent.com/pod-product-compliance
Lightning Source LLC
Chambersburg PA
CBHW042002100426

42813CB00020B/2961